LET'S EXPLORE THE STATES

Southwest

New Mexico
Oklahoma
Texas

Johnna M. Laird

Mason Crest
450 Parkway Drive, Suite D
Broomall, PA 19008
www.masoncrest.com

©2016 by Mason Crest, an imprint of National Highlights, Inc.

Printed and bound in the United States of America.

CPSIA Compliance Information: Batch #LES2015.
For further information, contact Mason Crest at 1-866-MCP-Book.

First printing
1 3 5 7 9 8 6 4 2

Library of Congress Cataloging-in-Publication Data

Laird, Johnna M.
  Southwest : New Mexico, Oklahoma, Texas / Johnna M. Laird.
    pages cm. — (Let's explore the states)
  Includes bibliographical references and index.
  ISBN 978-1-4222-3334-4 (hc : alk. paper)
  ISBN 978-1-4222-8619-7 (ebook : alk. paper)
  1. Southwestern States—Juvenile literature. 2. New Mexico—Juvenile literature.
  3. Oklahoma—Juvenile literature. 4. Texas—Juvenile literature. I. Title.
  F785.7.L35 2015
  976—dc23
                        2014050329

Let's Explore the States series ISBN: 978-1-4222-3319-1

About the Author: Johnna M. Laird writes for newspapers. She taught fourth grade for 17 years and loves working with and writing for children. Laird hails from the South with ties to Oklahoma and Texas. Her husband grew up in New Mexico. She lives in California with her husband and dog, Daisy.

Picture Credits: Office of the Governor of New Mexico: 19 (top); Library of Congress: 17, 18, 35, 41 (right), 56; National Aeronautics and Space Administration: 34; National Archives: 55; used under license from Shutterstock, Inc.: 1, 5 (bottom), 6, 7, 9, 10, 11, 12, 13, 14, 21, 23, 26, 27, 29, 30, 33, 37, 38, 39, 44, 45, 47, 48, 50, 57, 59 (right), 61; Andrey Bayda/Shutterstock.com: 20; Kobby Dagan / Shutterstock.com: 24; Featureflash/Shutterstock.com: 41 (left); Christopher Halloran/Shutterstock.com: 58; Meunierd/Shutterstock.com: 19 (bottom), 22; Nagel Photography / Shutterstock.com: 5 (top); Andrea Raffin/Shutterstock.com: 59 (left); Fara Spence/Shutterstock.com: 36; Texas State Library and Archives Commission: 53; Wikipedia Commons: 15.

Table of Contents

KEY ICONS TO LOOK FOR:

Words to Understand: These words with their easy-to-understand definitions will increase the reader's understanding of the text, while building vocabulary skills.

Sidebars: This boxed material within the main text allows readers to build knowledge, gain insights, explore possibilities, and broaden their perspectives by weaving together additional information to provide realistic and holistic perspectives.

Research Projects: Readers are pointed toward areas of further inquiry connected to each chapter. Suggestions are provided for projects that encourage deeper research and analysis.

Text-Dependent Questions: These questions send the reader back to the text for more careful attention to the evidence presented there.

Series Glossary of Key Terms: This back-of-the book glossary contains terminology used throughout this series. Words found here increase the reader's ability to read and comprehend higher-level books and articles in this field.

LET'S EXPLORE THE STATES

Atlantic: North Carolina, Virginia, West Virginia

Central Mississippi River Basin: Arkansas, Iowa, Missouri

East South-Central States: Kentucky, Tennessee

Eastern Great Lakes: Indiana, Michigan, Ohio

Gulf States: Alabama, Louisiana, Mississippi

Lower Atlantic: Florida, Georgia, South Carolina

Lower Plains: Kansas, Nebraska

Mid-Atlantic: Delaware, District of Columbia, Maryland

Non-Continental: Alaska, Hawaii

Northern New England: Maine, New Hampshire, Vermont

Northeast: New Jersey, New York, Pennsylvania

Northwest: Idaho, Oregon, Washington

Rocky Mountain: Colorado, Utah, Wyoming

Southern New England: Connecticut, Massachusetts, Rhode Island

Southwest: New Mexico, Oklahoma, Texas

U.S. Territories and Possessions

Upper Plains: Montana, North Dakota, South Dakota

The West: Arizona, California, Nevada

Western Great Lakes: Illinois, Minnesota, Wisconsin

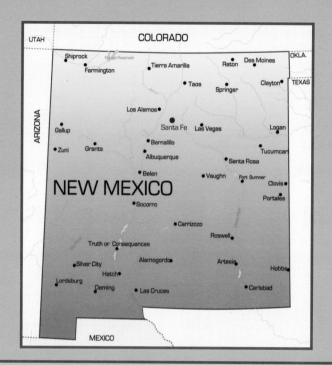

New Mexico at a Glance

Area: 121,590 sq miles (314,917 sq km)[1]. Fifth-largest state
  Land: 121,356 sq mi (314,411 sq km)
  Water: 234 sq mi (606 sq km)
Highest elevation: Wheeler Peak, 13,161 feet (4,012 m)
Lowest elevation: Red Bluff Reservoir 2,842 feet (866 m)

Statehood: Jan. 6, 1912 (47th state)
Capital: Santa Fe

Pop.: 2,085,572 (36th largest state)[2]

State nickname: Land of Enchantment
State bird: roadrunner
State flower: yucca

[1] U.S. Census Bureau
[2] U.S. Census Bureau, 2014 estimate

New Mexico

New Mexico beckons people outdoors for sports and recreation. People ski, snowboard, mountain bike, and hot air balloon. Spectacular mountains, riveting red canyons, glistening white sands, and limestone caverns make New Mexico nature's geologic wonderland. There are so many places to explore!

New Mexicans love their foods. They became the first to adopt an official cookie. New Mexico is also the only state with an official question: "Green or red?" The answer depends on whether the person prefers to eat red or green chilis with their food.

Geography

One of three southwestern states, New Mexico is box-shaped and *landlocked*. The state is 343 miles (550 km) wide and 370 miles (595 km) long. Colorado borders New Mexico to the north. Texas and the country of Mexico lock in the state to the south. Oklahoma, as well as part of Texas, lie

to the east, while Arizona borders New Mexico to the west.

New Mexico is the fifth-largest state in land size, but has the least surface water. Elephant Butte Lake is the state's largest lake, created by damming the Rio Grande River. More than a million people visit this reservoir each year for water recreation.

The Rio Grande River starts in Colorado and cuts through New Mexico before winding into Texas, where it forms the border between the United States and Mexico. It is the largest river in the state, and the fourth-longest river in North America.

The Chihuahuan Desert, the third-largest desert in the western hemisphere, covers much of central and southern New Mexico. Las Cruces

 Words to Understand in This Chapter

archaeologist—a person who studies bones, tools, and other items created by humans in the long-ago past.

civilization—a well-organized, developed human society.

commissioners—high-ranking members of a government organization who are assigned certain jobs.

conquistadors—Spanish soldiers who explored North and South America, seeking treasure and conquering the native people they encountered.

decimate—to destroy or kill a large number of people.

irrigate—to supply land or crops with water through man-made means.

landlocked—enclosed by land.

negotiate—to agree to something through discussion and consensus.

petition—a written document that many people sign to show that they want a person or organization to do or change something.

petroglyphs—rocks with carvings, drawings, or writing on them.

The Pecos River flows through the desert. The river originates in the Sangre de Cristo Mountains.

This grotto is located in Carlsbad Caverns National Park in southeastern New Mexico. The caves here formed over millions of years as acidic waters dissolved limestone. The park is in the Guadalupe Mountains at the end of the Chihuahuan Desert coming up from Mexico.

These tent-shaped formations, sometimes called hoodoos or tent rocks, were created by the erosion of volcanic rock over millions of years. This mountain is part of Kasha-Katuwe Tent Rocks National Monument in north-central New Mexico.

and Roswell are high desert cities located here.

Volcanic landforms pepper the state. Capulin Volcano National Monument, in northeastern New Mexico, gives visitors access to a cinder cone volcano. With so many accessible, extinct volcanoes to explore, New Mexico has received the unofficial nickname "Volcano State."

The Great Plains, one of four geographic regions in the state, stretches north to south over a high plateau. It extends over one-third of the eastern part of the state. The Pecos River, and others, cross this area. Over time, rivers carved deep canyons. Cattle and sheep are farmed in the north. Southward, land is used for dry and *irrigated* farming.

The Colorado Plateau in the northwest stretches across rugged land-

 Did You Know?

About 400,000 Mexican bats call Carlsbad Caverns home during the summer.

scape with canyons, cliffs and mesas. This region covers about one-fourth of the state. It includes Chaco Culture National Historical Park and Acoma Sky City, built on a mesa. A 40-mile (64 km) strip of volcanoes and lava plains, including El Malpais National Monument, lies in this region.

The Continental Divide extends through the Colorado Plateau and into the Basin and Range Region. The plateau includes Four Corners, where Arizona, Colorado, Utah and New Mexico come together.

The Rocky Mountains extend into central New Mexico. Wheeler Mountain, the state's highest peak, is located near Taos in the Sangre de Cristo Mountain Range. New Mexico's 100 highest peaks extend more than two miles above sea level. The Rio Grande winds its way through the Rocky Mountain region.

The Basin and Range Region extends south of the Rocky Mountains. Rugged mountain ranges characterize the region. These include the Guadalupe, Mogollon, Organ,

Shiprock is a stone formation that rises 1,580 feet (482 m) above the high plains near the Four Corners area where New Mexico, Arizona, Colorado, and Utah meet. It is located on the territory of the Navajo nation.

The Rio Grande Gorge Bridge is one of the highest bridges in the United States, rising 565 feet (172 m) above the river to the northwest of Taos.

History

Ancient people made their way into the land of New Mexico thousands of years ago. Artifacts found near Clovis place humans here at least 12,000 years ago. Near Capulin Volcano, **archaeologists** found evidence of a later group, the Folsom People. Like the Clovis People, the Folsom used stone tools and weapons.

Three advanced cultural groups later emerged in New Mexico: Hohokam, Mongollon, and Anasazi. Agriculture, architecture, population clusters, and social structure helped advance their societies.

Hohokam lived in smaller settlements in the Sonoran Desert near Gila River about 200 C.E. They developed irrigation systems to grow crops and trade with cultures to the south.

Mongollons settled into southern and western New Mexico around 150 C.E. Initially foragers, they began to rely more on farming.

Anasazi settled northward near the four corners. By 700 C.E., they built permanent dwelling places. In a remote northwestern desert, Anasazi

Sacramento, and San Andres. Three Rivers **Petroglyph** Site in this region preserves 21,000 rock art glyphs created by Jornada Mogollon people starting about 900 C.E.

developed the Chaco Culture in the mid- to late-800s. The site became a center for their *civilization*'s economy, administration, and ceremonies.

Chaco's monumental construction is described as North American Indians' greatest architectural feat. One building stood five stories. It occupied more than two acres of land and provided more than 2,500 rooms. Roads 30 feet wide radiated out from the buildings. Some scholars believe the roads linked to sacred, ceremonial sites. Others say they served as trade routes to Mexico, 600 miles away.

A severe drought struck the Southwest around 1130. By 1150, the buildings constructed with advanced masonry techniques were abandoned. People dispersed to the east and to the south.

Late arrivals like the Navajo and

People have lived in Acoma Sky City, built on a 367-foot tall mesa (a steep-sided, flat-topped hill), for nearly 1,000 years, making it the oldest continuously inhabited community in North America.

The Taos Pueblo has been inhabited by Native Americans for more than 1,000 years. It is located about a mile (1.6 km) north of the modern city of Taos. The United Nations has designated Taos Pueblo a "World Heritage Site." Inhabitants of the pueblo painted their doors blue, believing that this would prevent evil spirits from entering their homes.

Apache entered New Mexico as early as 1,000 years ago. Navajos followed the ways of the Anasazi, creating settlements and growing foods. The Apaches remained nomadic.

By the time Europeans arrived, about 80 different native communities lived in New Mexico. They included the Hopi and Zuni cultures.

The Spanish *conquistadors* brought horses and guns—technology that helped Europeans to conquer native people. They also brought an unintended weapon—diseases. Europeans had lived closely among each other and their domesticated animals. They built up immunities to measles and small pox. These diseases and others *decimated* the American Indians.

Estevanico, an enslaved scout, became the first African to step into New Mexico. He led the 1539 expedition from Mexico for priest Marcos de Niza. Niza was searching for Cibola, the fabled seven cities of gold. Zunis killed Estevanico. Fearful for his life, Niza returned to Mexico City and reported seeing one city of gold.

From 1540 to 1542, Francisco Vásquez de Coronado led an expedition of more than 1,000 soldiers and native guides throughout the Southwest, including New Mexico. He claimed land for Spain, but he found no evidence to support Niza's tales.

In 1581, Spanish explorers traveled the Rio Grande by water into New Mexico. Juan de Oñate followed in 1598 with a group of 130 soldiers, their families, and 10 priests to establish the first Spanish colony in New Mexico near the Chama River.

The Spanish treated the natives brutally, ousting them from their homes and demanding food and labor.

One tribe, the Acomas, fought back. They were slaughtered. Onate's men killed more than 800 men, women, and children. They punished survivors, enslaving most. The Spanish cut off the left foot of every man age 25 and older.

Don Pedro de Peralta arrived in 1610. He established Santa Fe as the New Mexico colony capital.

The Spanish worked to convert native people to Catholicism and make them loyal Spanish subjects. They promised if natives embraced

The Spanish explorer Juan de Oñate established the first European settlement in New Mexico at San Juan Pueblo, 25 miles (40 km) north of present-day Santa Fe.

Christianity, their crops would flourish. When crops failed, native leaders called for a return to traditional ways. In response, the Spanish hung three leaders. They whipped and imprisoned 43 others, including a military-minded leader, Popé.

When freed, Popé plotted for five years and gathered support from 17,000 people from villages hundreds of miles away. In August 1680, he led a revolt of united native people. More than 400 Spanish died. The Spanish who survived the Pueblo Revolt were driven out of New Mexico for a decade until Diego de Vargas *negotiated* a Spanish return in 1692.

In 1706, 30 Spanish families settled Albuquerque. The French arrived in the 1730s. Natives welcomed the French trade. Spaniards feared the French wanted to use New Mexico as a gateway to Mexican silver mines.

Conflicts between Comanches and Spaniards subsided in 1786 when the two groups negotiated a treaty allowing them to live in peace for 35 years.

In 1807, Zebulon Pike became the first American to explore New Mexico. He led a Southwest expedition to map the Red River.

By August 1821, Spain lost control of its colony. New Mexico then became a northern province of Mexico. Spain prevented trade with other countries, but Mexico welcomed traders. William Becknell of Missouri was among the first, blazing a trail in September 1821 from Missouri. He returned with more goods the next year along the Santa Fe Trail he helped to open.

War erupted between Mexico and the United States in 1846. By 1848, the U.S. won the conflict and acquired nearly half of Mexico's land, including present-day New Mexico, Arizona, California, Texas, Nevada and Utah.

New Mexicans prepared for statehood, but the Compromise of 1850 enacted by the U.S. Congress left New Mexico a territory. New Mexico, part of the Wild West, was a world away from Washington, D.C. Stagecoaches linked the distant territory to the rest of the country with mail service in 1857 until the railroads arrived. The first passengers traveling by train entered New Mexico in 1879 on the Atchison, Topeka and Santa Fe Railroad.

By 1888, New Mexico established its first public institution for higher learning, Las Cruces College. It became New Mexico College of Agriculture and Mechanic Arts, now New Mexico State University.

The Spanish-American War of

1898 may have helped boost New Mexico's path to statehood. Recruits from New Mexico proved U.S. loyalty by joining America's first volunteer cavalry. They gained fame as Rough Riders under Theodore Roosevelt's leadership. By 1910 President William H. Taft launched the statehood process. On January 6, 1912, New Mexico became the nation's 47th state. William C. McDonald became the state's first governor.

When national roads opened the state, Americans became better acquainted with New Mexico. In 1926, the "Mother Road," Route 66, crossed through Santa Fe, linking Chicago to Los Angeles. In 1960, Interstate 40 linked Atlantic and Pacific Coasts, bringing people through New Mexico.

Discovered in Hobbs in 1928, oil launched one of the state's most important industries.

During World War II, Navajo Code Talkers from New Mexico used 600 words of their ancient language to send coded messages. They transmitted vital secret communications for America without enemy interception.

Members of the 1st Volunteer Cavalry Regiment, better known as the Rough Riders, came from the southwest, particularly Arizona, New Mexico, Oklahoma, and Texas. The soldiers were drawn from this region because they were used to the sort of conditions they would face in Cuba during the Spanish-American War of 1898. They are pictured with Teddy Roosevelt, who was second in command of the regiment, after the Battle of San Juan Hill.

Surrounded by dignitaries, President William Howard Taft signs the bill admitting New Mexico as a state on January 6, 1912.

New Mexico gained world attention near the end of World War II. The top-secret Manhattan Project at Los Alamos National Laboratory developed an atomic weapon. Bombs dropped in 1945 on Hiroshima and Nagasaki, Japan, changed the world forever.

Back from World War II, Marine veteran and Native American Miguel Trujillo launched a successful lawsuit in 1948 to gain voting rights, denied many American Indians. By the 1960s, many Hispanic New Mexicans were speaking out for civil rights.

In 2011, Susana Martinez made history when she became the first woman to take office as governor of New Mexico.

Government

New Mexico's state capital, Santa Fe, is the oldest capital city in the country. New Mexico has the only round state capitol building in the U.S. The Roundhouse resembles the Zia Pueblo sun symbol found on the state's flag.

The executive branch, led by the governor, insures that state laws are implemented and enforced. Elected to a four-year term, the governor may serve two terms in a row.

The Senate and the House of Representatives comprise the lawmaking body, the state legislature. New Mexico voters elect 42 senators and 70 members of the House of Representatives. Senators serve four year terms; representatives serve two-year terms.

The legislature meets for 60 days in odd-numbered years and 30 days in even years. The governor and the legislature can call special sessions. Voters, through a referendum or *petition* process, can gather signatures to call for a vote to eliminate a law passed by the legislature. Legislation passed by the Senate and House of Representatives requires the governor's signature before becoming law. The governor has veto power and can refuse to sign a bill.

Susana Martinez is the first female governor of New Mexico. She also is the first Hispanic woman elected governor anywhere in the United States. Martinez was elected to a second term as governor in 2014, with 57 percent of the vote.

Five justices, elected to eight-year terms, serve on the State Supreme Court, the highest court in the state. Justices review and rule on decisions by lower courts. They elect their chief justice every two years.

Each of the state's 33 counties is governed by a county commission. *Commissioners* make laws and implement them. Commissioners hire a county manager to oversee day-to-day operations.

New Mexico's state capitol building in Santa Fe is distinctive because of its round shape. The building, known informally as "the roundhouse," includes offices and meeting halls for the state legislature. It was opened in 1966.

A Native American performs at an inter-tribal ceremony in Gallup. Today the state officially recognizes 22 tribes as sovereign nations, each with its own government, traditions, and culture. More than 220,000 Native Americans live in New Mexico today.

Native American tribes, recognized as sovereign nations by the federal government, also operate their own governments that negotiate and cooperate with U.S. government agencies.

New Mexicans elect two senators and three members of the House of Representatives to serve in the U.S. Congress in Washington, D.C.

The Economy

The federal government ranks as the top employer in the state. For every dollar the state collects in taxes, the federal government spends more than two dollars within the state. Tourism from within the United States generates nearly $6 billion annually and ranks as the top private or non-government employment.

While the state has no history of industrial-age factories, manufacturing is on the rise with production of computer parts and electronics.

The mining industry generates 80 percent of its revenue from petroleum and natural gas. New Mexico produces about 10 percent of the nation's natural gas, not surprising since it has one of the largest U.S. natural gas reserve fields in the southeastern part of the state. New Mexico produces about three percent of the nation's crude oil. From northwestern coal deposits, the state produces 90 percent of its electricity. Wind production powers more than 275,000 homes, making the state 17th in America's wind production.

Pastures occupy nearly 90 percent of the state's 43.2 million acres of

Albuquerque is one of the fastest-growing cities in the United States.

farmland. The state claims the nation's largest dairy herds. New Mexico ranks ninth in milk production and fourth in U.S. cheese production. Recent census figures show farming on the increase with 24,721 farms, up 18 percent over five years. Leading agricultural products include: dairy, beef cattle and calves; pecans, hay (to feed cattle and sheep), sheep, onions, chiles, greenhouse/nursery products, cotton, and corn. New Mexico ranks among America's top three pecan producers.

The People

Hispanics comprise the largest ethnic majority in New Mexico with 47 percent. Caucasians number 36 percent. About 10 percent of the state identifies as American Indian or Alaskan Native. Another two percent are African American. Asian, Hawaiian and other Pacific Islanders make up the rest of the state.

About 50 percent of the state reports that it is religious. About 29 percent identify as Catholic, the religion brought by the Spanish more than 400 years before.

American Indians are the ethnic group with the longest history in the state. New Mexico contains 19 pueblos and three reservations. The largest American Indian group in the U.S., the Navajo Nation, spreads over 27,000 miles in three states, including New Mexico.

Major Cities

At 7,000 feet above sea level in desert mountains, *Santa Fe* rises as the state capital with the nation's highest elevation. Founded in 1610, Santa Fe also ranks as the oldest U.S capital city and as New Mexico's fourth most populous city. Santa Fe attracts more than one million visitors annually.

With 100 art galleries clustered within a mile of each other, Santa Fe became America's first UNESCO Creative City. The Palace of

This adobe house, which is around 400 years old, still stands in Santa Fe. Today, Santa Fe's historic adobe structures can be found throughout the city.

Famous People from New Mexico

Jeffrey Preston "Jeff" Bezos (b. 1964) is founder and CEO of Amazon.com, the largest retailer on the World Wide Web. In 2013, Bezos bought the *Washington Post* newspaper for $250 million.

Geronimo (1829–1909) was an Apache leader who fought against Mexican and U.S. armies. He sought revenge after Mexican soldiers killed his wife and children. Born Goyathlay, he took the name Geronimo.

William Hanna (1910–2001) drew cartoon characters with his cartoonist partner, Joseph Barbera. They developed Tom and Jerry, Huckleberry Hound, Scooby Doo, and the Jetsons, among others.

Actor Neil Patrick Harris (b. 1973) starred in the television series *How I Met Your Mother*, in addition to other TV shows and movies like *Starship Troopers* (1997) and *Gone Girl* (2014).

Conrad Hilton (1887–1979) established the world's first international hotel chain. He owned 188 hotels in 38 U.S. cities.

Peter Hurd (1904–1984) was an American artist. He painted fresco murals over a two-year period, one per week. His portrait of President Lyndon B. Johnson currently hangs in the Smithsonian.

Neil Patrick Harris

Maria Martinez (1887–1980) became internationally known as a pottery artist. She worked to perfect blackware like pottery pots in the style created by the Pueblo people from 4,000 to 2,000 B.C.E. Martinez was born in New Mexico Territory.

Pro football quarterback Colt McCoy (b. 1986) is from Hobbes, while running back Arian Foster (b. 1986) was born in Albuquerque.

Georgia O'Keefe (1887–1986) is one of America's most important artists. She is known as the "Mother of Modernism."

Bill Richardson (b. 1947) was governor of New Mexico from 2003 to 2011. He has served in many other important positions, including U.S. Ambassador to the United Nations and as U.S. Secretary of Energy.

Bill Richardson

Each October, Albuquerque hosts the International Balloon Fiesta.

Governors, a government building that dates from the Spanish colonial era, houses 400 years of New Mexico's history. Known as "the City Different," Santa Fe blends American Indian, Spanish, Mexican, and Anglo Saxon cultures. Instead of skyscrapers, Santa Fe's skyline retains many adobe buildings, a tribute to its past.

Established in 1706, *Albuquerque* is New Mexico's most populous city with more than 556,000 residents. The Rio Grande passes through this city that spreads over 190 square miles. The metropolitan area's largest employer, Kirtland U.S. Air Force Base, conducts weapons research and ranks as the sixth largest military base in the world. Albuquerque is home to the University of New Mexico, Sandia Labs, and the world's largest hot air ballooning event.

Las Cruces, population 101,300, is New Mexico's second-largest city and part of the state's fastest-growing metropolitan area. It is home to New Mexico State University and White Sands Missile Range, the U.S. Army's largest military installation in the Western Hemisphere. NMSU and White Sands are the two largest area employers.

New Mexico's fifth largest city, *Roswell* (population 48,600), gained fame when a local paper carried the headline "RAAF Captures Flying Saucer on Ranch in Roswell Region" on July 8, 1947. Although the Air Force explained that the "saucer" was debris from an experimental weather balloon, interest in UFOs and extraterrestrials still brings tourists to Roswell.

Further Reading

Bjorklund, Ruth, and Ellen H. Todras. *It's My State! New Mexico*. New York: Cavendish Square, 2014.

Burgan, Michael. *New Mexico*. New York: Children's Press, 2009.

Internet Resources

www.nmstatelibrary.org/.../gi21_kids_handout

Kid Stuff Resources – New Mexico State Library (Government Information in the 21st Century)

http://www.nps.gov/safe/planyourvisit/places-to-go-in-new-mexico.htm

National Park Service

http://www.newmexicohistory.org/

Office of the State Historian

 # Text-Dependent Questions

1. Name New Mexico's longest river and locate it on a map.
2. Identify three ways in which Santa Fe is different from other capital cities.
3. What is the largest ethnic group in the state?

 # Research Project

Design a map, introducing seven natural wonders to explore in New Mexico. Use this book, the Internet, and your school library for research. List key information, location, and what makes each a point of interest. Evaluate your list to identify the top seven points of interest. Create a colorful map that would make you want to visit these sites. Present to classmates or post in your school library.

Oklahoma at a Glance

Area: 69,899 sq miles (181,037 sq km)[1]
  (20th largest state)
  Land: 68,595 sq mi (177,660 sq km)
  Water: 1,309 sq mi (3,377 sq km)
Highest elevation: Black Mesa, 4,973
  feet (1,516 m) above sea level
Lowest elevation: along Little River in
  McCurtain County, 287 feet (87 m)
  above sea level

Statehood: Nov. 6, 1907 (46th state)
Capital: Oklahoma City

Population: 3,878,051
  (28th largest state)[2]

State nickname: Sooner State
State bird: Scissor-tailed flycatcher
State flower: Mistletoe

[1] *U.S. Census Bureau*
[2] *U.S. Census Bureau, 2014 estimate*

Oklahoma

Native American culture thrives in Oklahoma. Festivals, museums, and heritage centers showcase traditions of 67 tribes that settled the state. About 100 Native American tribes converge in Oklahoma for the Red Earth Festival each year. The name *Oklahoma* itself comes from a Choctaw word meaning "Red People."

From a painful past, Native Americans have worked with other Oklahomans to create a state that has become a 21st century leader in the fields of technology, energy, and space.

Geography

The smallest Southwestern state, Oklahoma borders six states. Colorado and Kansas lie north, Texas south, Missouri and Arkansas east, and New Mexico and Texas west. Oklahoma spans 478 miles (769 km) east to west at its widest point, the northern border. From north to south, its eastern border runs 231 miles (372 km).

Oklahoma's shape makes it recognizable on a map. Some people say it looks like a jagged-edged butcher's cleaver; others say a pot with a handle. Oklahoma's narrow northwestern strip is called the Panhandle. Oklahoma has more diverse terrain than any other state. Eleven different *ecoregions* are found within five land regions of high *plains* (Great Plains), central lowlands, Ozark Plateau, the Ouachita, and coastal plain.

Oklahoma's Panhandle—166 miles (267 km) long and 34 miles (55 km) wide—lies in high plains with semi-arid, open spaces. Elevations rise from 2,000 to 4,973 feet (610 to 1,516 m) at Oklahoma's highest point, Black Mesa. Three counties make up the Panhandle, the state's least populated area, with less than one percent of the population. Wheat and hog farms thrive here. In the 1930s, the *Dust Bowl* struck here more severely than elsewhere in Oklahoma.

Oklahoma's Central Lowlands lie east of the Panhandle. They comprise more than half the state, covering central and western Oklahoma. This region stretches from Kansas to the

 Words to Understand in This Chapter

capitol—the building in which a legislative assembly meets.

Dust Bowl—central area of the United States in the 1930s where drought, farming practices, and wind storms created a disaster for tens of thousands farming families, who were forced to abandon their land when it could no longer be farmed.

ecoregion—areas with similar climate, geology, and soils which can lead to similarity in species.

export—to send goods to another country for sale; a product that is sent overseas.

plain—a large area of land that is flat or rolling, without trees.

sorghum—a grass; sorghum seeds feed cattle or can be used to make flour; USA is the largest sorghum producer in the world.

Buffalo graze on the prairie near Lawton in southwestern Oklahoma.

Red River. Farmers grow wheat primarily. They also grow cotton, peanuts, *sorghum*, and soybeans. Several ecoregions fit in this region: Gypsum Hills, Red Bed Plains, Sandstone Hills, Prairie Plains, and Tallgrass Prairie. Gypsum Hills in western Oklahoma rise to 700 feet (213 m), glistening like glass in sunlight. Red Beds Plains and Sandstone Hills hold oil fields and the state's economic centers, Tulsa and Oklahoma City. Oklahoma's coal deposits are concentrated in the Prairie Plain, where tall grasses once spanned this subregion. Oklahoma and Kansas are the only two states where the eight-foot tall grasses can still be seen. Nature Conservancy Tallgrass Prairie Preserve near Pawhuska is a good place for viewing tall grasses.

The pie-shaped Ozark Plateau lies at Oklahoma's far northeastern corner. Hay leads crop growth in this

A road runs through the Ouachita Mountain range, with trees covered in autumn leaves. This range stretches into central Arkansas.

region of hills, swift streams, and river-carved valleys. Forests are thick here. Grand Lake O' The Cherokees, a large lake, was created by the Pensacola Dam on the Grand River (lower Neosho River). This lake offers more than 1,300 shoreline miles for camping, bass fishing, and water sports. Pensacola Dam, Oklahoma's first hydroelectric dam with 51 arches, claims to be the world's largest multiple-arch dam.

The Ouachita lies south of the Ozark Plateau. One of four Oklahoma mountain ranges, the Ouachita is the tallest range between the Appalachian and Rocky Mountains. Tourists enjoy spectacular views and mineral springs here. Rainfall doubles that of western Oklahoma. Lumber mill towns developed here in the late 1800s, and timber remains an important industry in this region.

The Coastal Plain, adjacent to Arkansas and north of the Red River, lies south of the Kiamichi and Arbuckle Mountains. The nine-county region includes lakes that attract tourists. The timber and petroleum industries lead employment here.

The Wichita Mountains, comprised of granite, lie mostly within Fort Sill Military Reservation and a federal wildlife refuge in southwestern Oklahoma. The three major mountain ranges—Ouachita, Arbuckle, and Wichita—lie across the southern third of the state.

As the Red River alters course over time, Oklahoma and Texas have agreed to adjust their borders with the river, rather than argue. In 1999, the states agreed that the south bank of the river vegetation would serve as the official border.

History

Native Americans have lived in Oklahoma for thousands of years. Seen as primitive by Europeans, Native Americans developed sophisticated lifestyles. They adapted to the land. Evidence of prehistoric tribes places them in Oklahoma between 11,000 and 13,000 years ago. Some experts say it is likely humans lived here 20,000 to 30,000 years ago.

These nomadic hunter-gatherers used stone-age technology. They developed spearhead weaponry to kill large animals for food. As weather patterns changed, they settled into villages and grew plants for food. People who lived here were not one tribe, but several confederations. They developed trade systems and followed pantheistic religions.

The arrival of Europeans was a cataclysmic event for Native Americans. Europeans and Native Americans held different world views. Their cultures clashed. Diseases Europeans unintentionally brought eliminated 95 percent of the native people.

In 1540, Coronado claimed the Southwest for Spain. He returned to Mexico in 1542 without the gold he

 Did You Know?

Tattoos may seem like a 21st century phenomenon. The Wichitas or Kitikitish, a confederation of tribes living on the plains of Oklahoma, used them more than 1,000 years ago. Men tattooed their eyelids and women tattooed their chins.

had been searching for, and his trip was a costly failure.

In 1682, the French claimed Oklahoma as part of the vast Louisiana Territory. Louis Juchereau de St. Denis arrived in Oklahoma in 1714 followed by Jean-Baptiste Benard de La Harpe in 1718. They set up trading posts for fur trappers along the Red River.

In 1762, the French government turned over control of the Louisiana Territory to Spain, but the region came back under French control in 1801. The French government then agreed to sell this vast territory to the United States in 1803.

Over the next two decades, the U.S. explored the lands acquired through the Louisiana Purchase, organizing them into smaller territories. By 1819, the Arkansas Territory included Oklahoma, except for the Panhandle. That territory was given to Spain (which at the time controlled the American Southwest, including Texas) to settle a boundary dispute. Gradually, small numbers of white settlers trickled into Oklahoma.

Settlement in other parts of the U.S. played an important role in Oklahoma's history. In 1830, the U.S. government ordered Native Americans living in Georgia, Florida, Alabama, and South Carolina to leave their homes and move to a new "Indian Territory" in Oklahoma. Moving the tribes allowed whites to settle in other parts of those states.

Some Native Americans remained behind, assimilating into the European culture and becoming U.S. citizens. Thousands, however, traveled hundreds of miles to Oklahoma between 1831 and 1842. For the Cherokee, the trip became known as the "Trail of Tears." They were forced from their land. More than 4,000 Cherokee died on the journey.

 Did You Know?

The Thomas Gilcrease Museum in Tulsa is said to be the world's largest and most comprehensive collection of fine art, artifacts, and archives telling the story of the American West.

This map of Indian Territory from around 1880 shows the various tribal lands in the state. The Native American tribes that were resettled in Oklahoma included the five "civilized tribes" (the Cherokee, Chickasaw, Choctaw, Creek, and Seminole) who had come from the southeastern U.S. on the Trail of Tears, as well as other tribes from elsewhere on the Great Plains, such as the Arapaho, Cheyenne, Comanche, Kiowa, and Osage.

In Oklahoma, native tribes established their own governments. They believed the treaties would ensure their right to the land forever. They were wrong.

During the American Civil War (1861–65), some Cherokee and Chocktaw fought on the side of the Confederacy. After the war, these tribes were punished for supporting the rebels. Treaties were rewritten, and Native Americans lost some of their land. They also had to allow railroads to be built through their territories.

Throughout the 1870s and 1880s, white settlers continued to move west into Indian lands. The U.S. government removed the Plains Indians from their homes and forced them onto reservations in the Indian Territory to make room for the settlers. But Americans even wanted to settle in the Indian Territory. Eventually, the U.S. government purchased 3 million acres (1.21 million ha) in Indian Territory from the Creek and Seminole nations.

At noon on April 22, 1889, the government opened 1.9 million acres in Oklahoma to settlement. Within hours, the territory's population expanded by 50,000 people. Present-day Oklahoma City attracted 10,000

Oklahomans and the Space Program

The state of Oklahoma has strong ties to the U.S. space program, as many of America's groundbreaking astronauts were born here or grew up in the state.

L. Gordon Cooper (1927–2004) was one of the original seven American astronauts chosen in 1959. He flew in space for Project Mercury in 1961, becoming the fifth American to orbit the Earth. At the time, his 34-hour spaceflight was the longest any human had ever been in space. He later spent even longer—eight days—in space as commander of Gemini 5.

Gordon Cooper

Fred Haise (b. 1933) was supposed to land on the moon in 1970, but during the flight an explosion damaged his Apollo 13 spacecraft. The moon mission was aborted, but Haise and two other astronauts returned to Earth safely. Haise later helped to test the space shuttle.

Thomas Stafford (b. 1930) flew on two Gemini space flights, commanded the Apollo 10 mission that orbited the moon, and in 1975 commanded a mission with American and Soviet astronauts called Apollo-Soyuez.

Thomas Stafford

William Pogue (1930–2014) spent 84 days in space on Skylab, the first American space station.

Shannon Lucid (b. 1943) was among the first six female astronauts selected by NASA in 1978. She flew five missions in space. In 1996, on her final mission, she spent 188 days on the Russian space station *Mir*, setting a record. Lucid later served as Chief Scientist of NASA. She retired in 2012.

Shannon Lucid

John Herrington (b. 1958), a Chickasaw, was the first member of a Native American tribe to fly in space.

Carole Ann McElmore (b. 1960), a NASA engineer, helped design the International Space Station.

John Herrington

This painting depicts a frenzied "land rush," as settlers race to claim homesteads in the Oklahoma Territory in April 1889.

people before nightfall. So did Guthrie.

Some settlers could not wait. They grabbed land before the official starting time. These people became known as Sooners and gave Oklahoma its nickname.

Guthrie became the first capital of the Territory of Oklahoma in May 1890. The territory included the Panhandle, which had been acquired from Spain after the Mexican-American War in 1848.

Native American land ownership changed again in the 1890s. The Dawes Commission took away tribal lands altogether, instead dividing the territories among individual Native Americans. This opened additional Oklahoma land to settlement by whites. More than 50,000 settlers rushed into north central Oklahoma on September 16, 1893, to claim six million acres (2.43 ha) that had previously been owned by the Cherokee, Tonkawa, and Pawnee tribes.

In 1905, the Five Civilized Tribes' leaders met with white citizens in

Muskogee to create a Native American state. Congress rejected the idea and called for a single state uniting the "Twin Territories."

Native American leaders and white settlers later convened in Guthrie to draft a constitution. On November 16, 1907, Oklahoma became the 46th state. About 1.4 million people lived in Oklahoma at the time. Initially, Guthrie was the capital, but in 1910 the government moved to Oklahoma City.

At statehood, Oklahoma was already the nation's largest oil producer. Oil was discovered in Chelsea in 1889 and in Bartlesville in 1897. Oil

A memorial to the victims of the 1995 Oklahoma City bombing was built at the site of the Alfred P. Murrah Federal Building. These chairs represent the 168 adults and children killed in the terrorist attack.

was discovered in Tulsa in 1901. The Oklahoma City oil field began production in 1928. By 1940, more than 1,500 wells operated in Oklahoma.

The Great Depression began in 1929. It lasted a decade. It caused hardship for Oklahomans when banks failed. Financial hardships mounted from droughts that left the plains like a Dust Bowl. More than 250,000 people, most from Oklahoma, left the Southwest between 1935 and 1940. Many moved to California, where they became known by the derogatory term "Okies."

By the 1950s, farming declined. The state moved toward industry as its economic base. Oklahoma attracted electronics plants.

In the 1960s and 1970s, the state built lakes and dams to harness hydroelectric power. Oklahoma became a state with water, electric power, and fossil fuel resources.

Shipping became an important industry to this land-locked state in the 1970s. Oklahoma developed waterways to create river ports in Tulsa and Muskogee.

Tragedy brought world attention to Oklahoma on April 19, 1995. A truck bomb exploded outside the Alfred P. Murrah Federal Building in Oklahoma City. The blast killed 168 people and injured another 850. It damaged 300 downtown buildings. A memorial built on the site features sculpted, lighted chairs—one chair for each person killed in the bombing.

In 2011, Mary Fallin was elected the state's first female governor.

Government

Sooners send two U.S. senators to Washington, D.C., to represent them in Congress. They send five members to the U.S. House of Representatives.

Like the federal government, Oklahoma operates with three government branches: executive, legislative, and judicial.

The governor heads the executive branch. The governor is elected to four-year terms and may not serve more than two terms in a row. The executive branch insures that state laws are implemented and enforced. Sooners elect a lieutenant governor, state attorney general, treasurer, auditor, and superintendent of instruction to four-year terms. The governor, however, appoints

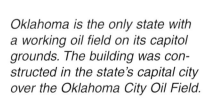

Oklahoma is the only state with a working oil field on its capitol grounds. The building was constructed in the state's capital city over the Oklahoma City Oil Field.

the secretary of state, and the state senate must confirm the nomination.

The legislative branch recommends and adopts laws. Lawmakers in the State House of Representatives and the Senate propose bills. A majority of members in each house must approve a bill before sending it to the governor to become law. The governor may sign or veto the bill. With a two-thirds majority vote in each house, the legislature can override a governor's veto.

Oklahoma has 101 State House of Representatives members, who are elected to two-year terms. The people elect 48 senators to four-year terms. Legislators represent geographic areas of Oklahoma. Legislators can serve for a maximum of 12 years in the state assembly.

The State Supreme Court, the highest court in the state, operates with nine justices. This includes a chief justice. The governor appoints justices to the bench, but Oklahoma voters must approve justices to remain on the bench. They serve six-year terms. The courts operate as a tiered system. There are municipal and district courts at the lowest levels and courts of appeal for both the criminal and civil courts.

Longhorn cattle graze in the Wichita Mountains of Oklahoma. Cattle ranching is an important part of the state's economy, and the state has more than 55,000 beef farms and ranches with a total of 4.5 million head of cattle.

With a population of 610,000, Oklahoma City is the 29th-largest city in the United States. The city covers more than 621 square miles (1,608 sq km), making it the fifth-largest American city by area.

Commissioners govern each of Oklahoma's 77 counties. County commissioners enact laws and oversee county services. Oklahoma's 600 cities and towns operate either a council and city manager form of government or a council and mayor system.

The Economy

Oklahoma ranks as the third-largest natural gas producer in the United States. It ranks fifth in oil production.

Petroleum and gas can be found across the state. Coal lies in the northeast and in the Arkansas Valley. Oklahoma is the only state with working oil drills on its *capitol* grounds. Nearly 350,000 jobs indirectly relate to the oil and gas industry. Another 85,000 are directly linked.

Employment in mining and mining-related jobs is expected to increase by about 20 percent over the next eight years. In 2013, nearly 15 percent of the state's electricity came from wind power.

Oklahoma also manufactures machinery for the operation of its gas fields and oil wells. This machinery is manufactured in several cities in Oklahoma. Manufacturers also produce equipment for farms, transportation, aerospace, and computers. Oklahoma ranks 38th in U.S. *exports* to other countries.

Nationwide, Oklahoma ranks fifth among all the states in beef cattle production, and eighth in hog production. Oklahoma ranchers and farmers also market chickens and eggs, dairy products, sheep and lambs, turkeys and farmed-raised catfish. Farms occupy three-fourths of Oklahoma's land.

Wheat is the state's largest field crop. Oklahoma ranks as the nation's fourth-largest wheat producer. Oklahoma leads the nation in production of another grain, rye.

Sales of Oklahoma agricultural products are not just within the U.S. Oklahoma exports agricultural products worth billions to other countries, including Canada and Mexico.

More Oklahomans today work in service industries than any other economic sector. Service industries include government. Government is the leading state employer. Unemployment in Oklahoma is lower than the U.S. average.

The People

A friendly and resilient people, Sooners embrace the idea that working can solve problems. The state motto is *Labor omnia vincit*, Latin for "Labor conquers all things."

Caucasians comprise 67 percent of the state's 3.8 million population. Hispanics make up about 10 percent. African Americans are 8 percent. About 2 percent are Asian. Native American and Alaskan are 9 percent. Due in part to its legacy as the Indian Territory, Oklahoma contains the nation's second-greatest Native American population after California.

About 25 percent of Oklahoma's population is under age 18. About 14 percent is over age 65.

Viewed as a swing state in the past, Oklahoma today is seen as conserva-

Famous People from Oklahoma

Folksinger Woodrow "Woody" Guthrie (1912–1967) wrote more than 1,000 songs, including "This Land Is Your Land." This is considered the third most popular song of the 20th century.

Mickey Mantle (1931–1995) hit 536 home runs during his 18 seasons with the New York Yankees. He was named MVP three times and played in 16 All-Star games. He was elected to the Baseball Hall of Fame in 1974.

Wilson Rawls (1913–1984) was best known for his award-winning books for children, such as *Where the Red Fern Grows* (1961) and *Summer of the Monkeys* (1976).

Will Rogers

Will Rogers (1879–1935) was a humorist and political commentator. He served as the voice of the "common man" during the 1920s and 1930s. He appeared in 70 Hollywood films.

Elizabeth Maria Tallchief (b. 1925) danced as a prima ballerina, traveling the world to perform. The Kennedy Center honored her in 1996.

Jim Thorpe (1888–1953) is widely considered the 20th century's greatest athlete. He won gold medals in the 1912 Olympics. He also played baseball and football professionally.

Jim Thorpe

Garth Brooks

Many country music singers have ties to Oklahoma. Tulsa native Garth Brooks (b. 1962) has sold more than 190 million albums worldwide, making him one of the best-selling solo artists of all time. Carrie Underwood (b. 1983), a native of Muskogee, has received many awards since winning the fourth season of *American Idol* in 2005. She was inducted into the Oklahoma Music Hall of Fame in 2009. Other notable country artists include Vince Gill (b. 1957), Toby Keith (b. 1961), Reba McEntire (b. 1955), and Blake Shelton (b. 1976).

tive. Sooners report themselves as more religious than the rest of the nation (59 percent to 49 percent).

Major Cities

Oklahoma City serves as the state capital. It is Oklahoma's largest city and a major work center for the state. Major employers include companies in the aviation and aerospace industries, bioscience, health care, manufacturing, energy, wholesale and retail trade, and in professional, business and financial services.

Tulsa is Oklahoma's second-largest city, with a population of 398,121. At one time, the city was called the "oil capital of the world." Today, Tulsa is home to more than 300 aerospace-related industries.

In 1970, the Tulsa Port of Catoosa linked Tulsa to the Mississippi River and the Gulf of Mexico. This opened the city to exports and imports from all over the world.

Less than 20 minutes outside Oklahoma City, *Norman* is Oklahoma's third-largest city (population 118,197). Railroads sparked the expansion and development of Norman. The city became home to Oklahoma's first institution of higher learning. The University of Oklahoma opened in 1895 with 100 students.

Oklahoma's higher education system today is comprised of 25 public colleges and universities. Included are 12 community colleges, 10 regional universities, two research universities and a public liberal arts university.

Further Reading

Baldwin, Guy and Hart, Joyce. *Celebrate the States: Oklahoma*. New York: Marshall Cavendish Benchmark, 2010.

Horn, Geoffrey M., and Doug Sanders. *It's My State! Oklahoma*. New York: Cavendish Square, 2014.

Internet Resources

http://www.ou.edu/cas/archsur/home.htm

The Oklahoma Archaeological Survey's website provides information about the ancient history of the state, as well as the native people who lived there before the arrival of Europeans.

http://digital.library.okstate.edu/encyclopedia/
http://www.okhistory.org/kids/index

These two sites, operated by the Oklahoma Historical Society, provide information about the state's history and culture.

https://www.census.gov/schools/facts/oklahoma.html

Facts and statistics about Oklahoma from the U.S. Census Bureau.

 # Text-Dependent Questions

1. Which major river runs the length of Oklahoma's southern border?
2. Where was the first oil field in Oklahoma?
3. Where is the University of Oklahoma located? What year did classes begin?
4. Oklahoma was once a swing state, where voters shifted back and forth in support of the two major political parties. Where does Oklahoma stand now?

 # Research Project

The Dust Bowl is referred to as "one of the worst man-made ecological disasters in American history." Why did it occur? Using the Internet and your school library, find out why the Dust Bowl occurred. How can learning about its the causes guide future actions? Write a two-page report on your findings and present it to your class.

Texas
at a Glance

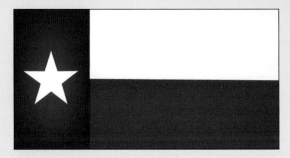

(2nd largest state)[2]

Area: 268,596 sq mi (695,662 sq km)[1]
(2nd largest state)
Land: 261,232 sq mi (676,587 sq km)
Water: 7,364 sq mi (19,075 sq km)
Highest elevation: Guadalupe Peak,
8,751 feet (2,667 m)
Lowest elevation: sea level (0 feet)

Statehood: Dec. 29, 1845 (28th state)
Capital: Austin

Population: 26,956,958

State nickname: Lone Star State
State bird: mockingbird
State flower: bluebonnet

[1] U.S. Census Bureau
[2] U.S. Census Bureau, 2014 estimate

Texas

Texans say "everything is bigger in Texas." A super-sized state—the largest by area of the 48 *contiguous* states—Texas produces more wool, more crude oil, more electricity, more windpower, and more rodeos than any other state. Texas boasts the world's largest rose garden. The dome on its pink granite capitol building rises seven feet higher than the U.S. Capitol. No wonder Texans say everything is bigger. Texas has five of America's top ten fastest growing cities.

Texas is the only state to join the United States after existing as an independent nation for several years. Maybe that's why Texans feel their state is "a whole other country."

Geography

The largest of three Southwestern states, Texas covers 268,596 square miles (695,662 square kilometers). Texas ranks as the second-largest state in the United States. Only Alaska encompasses more land.

Texas is so vast the entire New England region of six states, plus four more—

Pennsylvania, Ohio, Illinois and New Jersey—would fit inside. A walk around the state's borders—3,822 miles (6,151 km)—exceeds the distance from the Pacific Coast to the Atlantic. Texas comprises 7 percent of the total U.S. area, making it larger than many nations.

Four states border Texas: Arkansas and Louisiana to the east, Oklahoma to the north and New Mexico to the west. The Rio Grande River forms the state's southwest border with Mexico. The Gulf of Mexico forms Texas' southeast border and provides 367 miles (591 km) of beach coastline.

Texas land varies and is often seen as four regions: Gulf Coast Plains, North Central Plains, Great Plains, and the Mountain and Basin region.

Rolling and hilly plains characterize the Gulf Coast Plains region. This eastern-most region comprises about a third of the state. It includes a pine belt with 12 million acres (4.86 million hectares) of timberland. Grain, cotton, and citrus crops grow here in a sub-region, the Texas Coastal Prairies.

Words to Understand in this Chapter

barrier island—a long sandy island that runs parallel to the mainland and provides protection from the ocean.

contiguous—something that touches, or is connected to, something else.

empresarios—land agents who received Mexican government grants and recruited settlers to colonize Mexican lands.

escarpment—a cliff-like ridge formed by erosion or faulting.

lawlessness—a situation of disorder when laws go unenforced.

Texians—a word used to refer to citizens of Anglo-Americans areas and to citizens of the Republic of Texas in the 19th century. After 1845, it was replaced by the word "Texans."

Caddo Lake is one of the few natural lakes in Texas and is the second-largest lake in the South. This internationally protected wetland is home to bald cypress trees like the ones pictured here

Padre Island National Seashore is the world's longest undeveloped stretch of barrier island.

Cotton is ready to be picked on a farm in southern Texas. Texas produces about 4.5 million bales of cotton a year, more than any other state.

The Rio Grande river flows through Big Bend National Park. This river marks the border between Texas and Mexico.

El Capitan is a high peak in the Guadalupe Mountain range in west Texas. It rises 285 ft (87 m) above the surrounding terrain, and 8,064 feet (2,458 m) above sea level.

Cattle production creates an important money-maker. More land in Texas is devoted to grazing cattle than for any other use. King Ranch, begun more than 160 years ago and larger than the state of Rhode Island, is located in this region along with Texas' most populous cities—Dallas, Austin, Houston, and San Antonio. About two-thirds of the state's population live or work in this region. Gulf of Mexico breezes keep the weather warmer in winter and cooler in summer.

In the North Central Plains, south of the Red River, elevations rise with rolling and rugged hills. The Balcones Fault and *Escarpment* forms the boundary between this region and the Coast Plains. An earthquake millions of years ago lifted the land to create a long cliff that resembles balconies, explaining why the Spanish chose the name Balcones.

The Great Plains region looks a bit like an old-fashioned boot, extending from Texas's panhandle straight down the state and turning eastward. Elevations rise from 700 to 4,000 feet (210 to 1,220 m) above sea level. Panhandle farmers lead in state production of wheat, cotton, and grain sorghum. The Permian Basin here holds rich petroleum gas. On the Edwards Plateau to the south, farmers raise more sheep and goats than anywhere else in the United States.

The Mountain and Basin Region, western-most and called Trans-Pecos, includes Davis, Chisos, and Guadalupe Mountains. Guadalupe Peak at 8,751 feet (2,667 m) stands as Texas' highest peak. Big Bend, Texas' first and largest national park, boasts 800,000 acres (323,750 ha) of ecologically-valuable desert along the Rio Grande. The park safeguards 1,400 archaeological sites. The Rio Grande and Pecos Rivers flow through this area, Texas' driest and windiest region.

Texas' longest river is the Rio Grande. Red River, bordering Oklahoma, and the Canadian River, both flow eastward from the Panhandle. The Sabine River divides Texas from Louisiana, and like the Colorado, Brazos, and Trinity Rivers, flows south into the Gulf of Mexico. Smaller rivers dominate the Coastal Plains. Dammed rivers create about 200 lakes in the state.

History

About 11,500 years ago, the descendants of people who entered North America from Asia settled in Texas. Four different cultural groups of Native Americans emerged in the region: the Southeastern (Caddo), the Gulf Coast, Pueblo, and the Plains.

The Caddo were the largest and most advanced group. They lived in permanent structures built in southeastern Texas's pine forests. The Caddo raised crops like corn, beans, and squash, and hunted animals. The Caddo group included more than 25 tribes. They created a confederation of tribes called the Tejas, which meant "those who are friends." Texas takes its name from the word *tejas*.

Other native people included the Jumanos, who were peaceful traders and bison hunters. They traded with Southeastern tribes and Pueblo cliff dwellers.

The Spanish introduced horses to the region in the 16th century, and the Plains Indians became powerful hunters and warriors on horseback. In Texas, these tribes included the Apache and Comanche.

The arrival of the Spanish had a significant negative impact on the native people. Conquistadors arrived to claim native-occupied lands for Spain and plunder their riches. Spanish padres, or priests, arrived to convert native people to Catholicism and Spain's way of life.

In 1519, Alonso Álvarez de Pineda became the first European to explore the coast of Texas. He planned to establish a settlement but died in Mexico before he could return.

Álvar Núñez Cabeza de Vaca and Estevanico, an African slave, stumbled onto Texas shores in 1528 after their ship wrecked in a storm. Estevanico and Cabeza de Vaca spent years wandering through the Southwest. When

The Spanish brought horses to North America, and Native American tribes like the Comanche soon recognized their value. Use of the horse for hunting buffalo, as well as for warfare, revolutionized the lives of the nomadic Plains tribes. The Comanche were the largest and most dominant tribe in Texas until the 19th century.

they finally reached Spanish settlements in Mexico, they retold stories they had heard about a golden city, Cibola.

In 1540, seeking the golden city, Francisco Vásquez de Coronado led a small army into the Southwest. Coronado found Cibola, but it did not contain the riches he thought. Instead, it was a mud village of the Zuni people. Coronado continued to explore the Southwest for two more years, but his quest for wealth ultimately failed.

Sailing for France, Rene-Robert Cavelier, Sieur de La Salle and his men navigated the Mississippi River in 1682. They established Fort Saint Louis on a riverbank inland from the Texas coast. The settlement failed, but France gained a toehold in the New World for fur-trading.

Spain built its first mission settlement in west Texas in 1682 near present-day El Paso. Seeing France as a threat, Spaniards built San Francisco de los Tejas in 1690, in east Texas to buffer Mexico from French-held lands. More missions followed.

The first missions failed. Drought killed crops. European diseases killed large numbers of natives. Natives grew resentful of authority imposed by Catholic priests.

In 1821, Mexico gained independence from Spain. Claiming Texas, Mexico eliminated many Spanish practices. Spain's legacy remained through architecture and language. Several Texas cities, rivers, and streets still retain Spanish names.

During Spain's rule over Mexico, Moses Austin gained Spain's permission to establish a colony of 300 families in Texas. He died before he realized his plan. His son, Stephen F. Austin, age 27, led the first Anglo-American settlement of Texas, with the new Mexican government's approval.

Empresarios brought immigrants into Texas, and Austin was the most successful. His ability to speak both English and Spanish proved invaluable. Land given to him in exchange for recruiting settlers became the city of Austin.

For a while, Mexico welcomed colonists, who became known as

Texians. As the governmental ruling party changed, Mexico banned immigration. Colonists resented this and other regulation. Tensions increased.

Texians held conventions in 1832 and 1833 calling for change. Stephen Austin traveled to Mexico and gained concessions from the Mexican ruler General Antonio López de Santa Anna but not statehood.

Texans consider October 2, 1835, in Gonzales as the revolution's first battle for independence. Settlers fought against Mexican soldiers who demanded their town's cannon. Outnumbered, the Mexicans retreated. Fueled by success, the colonists took Goliad's garrison a week later. Colonists defeated a Mexican army of 1,000 on December 9, 1835, in San Antonio. Mexicans surrendered and returned home. Colonists returned home, believing the war had ended.

An interim Texas government established in November 1835 officially pledged support for Mexico but opposed a dictatorship. Delegates chose Sam Houston to head a paid army and Austin to gain U.S. support for Texas. Bickering over independence continued. Another convention was set for March 1836.

Santa Anna and his army arrived in San Antonio in February 1836. He kept about half of his 6,000 troops and sent others to the north. Houston wanted the Texians to abandon San Antonio. Instead, they prepared to defend the Spanish mission there, known as the Alamo.

On March 2, convention delegates meeting at Washington-on-the-Brazos declared independence. They wrote a constitution using some Mexican laws. The constitution allowed men and women to jointly hold property but banned freed slaves from living in Texas. Delegates approved the constitution on March 16. A day later they learned that Santa Anna was marching northward. They adjourned.

At the Alamo, Colonel William B. Travis, with less than 200 men, held off Mexican soldiers for 13 days. Early on the morning of March 6, 1836, Mexican soldiers climbed the Alamo's walls, overpowering and outnumbering the Texians. About 183 defenders

This painting, titled "Dawn at the Alamo," depicts the chaos inside the fort's walls when the Mexicans attacked early on the morning of March 6, 1836. On the north wall (at right), Alamo commander William Travis fires his pistol at an attacker. Travis was killed defending the wall, along with Davy Crockett, Jim Bowie, and about 180 other Texian defenders who died not knowing independence had been declared.

died, while roughly 600 Mexicans were killed.

In Goliad, Mexican soldiers surrounded 300 retreating Texians. The Texians surrendered, expecting fair treatment, but they were executed. "Remember Goliad" and "Remember the Alamo" became rallying cries for Texas independence.

A surprise attack by Houston and his army led to Santa Anna's capture and an end to war on April 21 at San Jacinto. In an 18-minute battle, the Texians took 730 prisoners and killed more than 600 Mexican soldiers. Santa Anna agreed to order Mexican troops out of Texas.

The Republic of Texas elected Sam Houston its first president in September 1836. Texians approved a constitution and moved to join the U.S. The path to statehood was complicated, however. Mexico did not recognize Texas' independence. The U.S. did not want to upset Mexico by annexing Texas.

In 1845, Texas joined the U.S. as the 28th state. A new state constitution outlined three branches of government and permitted slavery.

In 1846, the U.S. and Mexico went to war over Texas's boundary. The

Did You Know?

Because so many German immigrants settled in central Texas, the German language was widely spoken there from the 1840s until the 1970s.

United States ultimately won the Mexican-American War. The Treaty of Guadalupe Hidalgo, signed in 1848, placed the Texas-Mexico boundary at the Rio Grande. It also gave California, Arizona, New Mexico, and Texas to the U.S., along with portions of Utah, Nevada and Colorado,

In 1861, Texas joined the Confederacy as the seventh state to secede from the Union. Texas itself saw few battles, but about 60,000 Texans served in the Confederacy and 2,000 with the Union army.

The last battle of the Civil War was fought in Brownsville, Texas, on May 13, 1865, a month after the war ended because word of Robert E. Lee's surrender had not yet reached Texas. Union soldiers arrived on June 19, 1865, in Galveston to announce freedom for 250,000 slaves living in Texas.

Turmoil and *lawlessness* characterized post-Civil War Reconstruction in Texas, despite the federal government's military rule. Lynch mobs terrorized African Americans and some Mexican Americans.

Five years after the war, Texans wrote another constitution to rejoin the Union. In 1876, Texans created their sixth constitution. It limited the governor's powers, created the University of Texas, and established local control of schools. Although designed for a rural population, this constitution still guides the state today, although it has been amended more than 480 times.

Brought by Spaniards and bred by ranchers, longhorn cattle became important currency in Texas from 1866 to 1885. Ranchers moved thousands of cattle northward in drives to Missouri and Kansas railroads to gain higher prices in eastern markets. Cattle was second only to cotton among Texas's exports.

Texas changed in the early 1900s.

A steamboat is loaded with supplies at Fort Ringgold, Texas, on the Rio Grande river. It was headed to Brownsville. This photo was taken around 1890.

A September 1900 hurricane killed 10,000 people, devastating Galveston, an important financial center of the South. Oil drillers launched the modern petroleum industry four months later. At Spindletop near Beaumont, oil shot 100 feet in the air. Spindletop generated 100,000 barrels of oil daily. During the early 1900s, petroleum and gas production replaced agriculture as the basis of Texas's economy.

When the U.S. entered World War I in 1917, military training camps opened in Houston, Fort Worth, Waco, and San Antonio. Texas prospered during the war, with factories producing many items needed by the military. City populations grew by more than 50 percent. Homes welcomed electricity.

As in other states in the South, African Americans and Mexicans suffered from racial discrimination. Poll taxes made it impossible for most blacks and Latinos to vote. During the 1920s and 1930s, an African American doctor named Lawrence Nixon challenged the laws that kept blacks from voting. The U.S. Supreme Court ultimately ruled in his favor.

As in other Southwestern states, the Great Depression and the

A "gusher" erupts at Spindletop, the first major oil field discovered in Texas. The 1901 discovery of oil at Spindletop would revolutionize the U.S. oil industry and turn Texas from a rural, sparsely populated state of cattle ranches to a highly industrialized center with growing cities.

droughts that led to the Dust Bowl of the 1930s led many people to leave the state and find work elsewhere. Texas's fortunes improved during World War II, as the government built military bases, and industries expanded to meet the need for weapons and other supplies.

Texas modernized and expanded its system of higher education through the 1960s. The state used some of its oil revenue to create a comprehensive plan for higher education. These changes helped Texas universities receive federal research funds.

On November 22, 1963, President John F. Kennedy was assassinated in Dallas. His vice president, Lyndon B. Johnson, became president, and was elected to his own term in 1964. Johnson had previously represented Texas in the U.S. Senate from 1949 to 1961. Among his accomplishments was getting NASA's Manned Spacecraft Center built in Houston. The facility served as Mission Control for NASA's moon landings and for later space shuttle missions. It is now known as the Johnson Space Center.

In the 1970s, a series of oil crises

led to increased prices. This in turn led to an economic boom in Texas in the late 1970s and early 1980s. When prices fell in the mid-1980s, it wiped out many paper fortunes and led to a decline in the real estate and banking industries.

In 2000, former Texas governor George W. Bush was elected the 43rd president of the United States. Bush served two terms as president.

In 2014, a nurse at a Texas hospital became the first person in the U.S. infected with the Ebola virus, drawing national attention. The nurse became sick after treating a West African man who had been infected in his native country. Although the nurse recovered, the case sparked national fears about Ebola, a deadly infectious disease.

Government

The government of Texas is broken into executive, legislative, and judicial branches. The governor heads the executive branch. Elected by voters to serve a four-year term, the governor can serve an unlimited number of terms. The state constitution empowers the governor to appoint the secretary of state and the adjunct general. Voters elect other positions in the

During the oil boom of the early 1980s, many new skyscrapers were built in downtown Dallas. Over time, the oil industry in Texas has become centered around Houston, while Dallas and its suburbs have attracted technology companies. Some of the high-tech firms based in the state today include Texas Instruments, Dell Computer, and Verizon, while companies like Hewlett-Packard, AMD, and IBM have manufacturing facilities in Texas.

Rick Perry retired as governor of Texas in early 2015, after serving in that position longer than anyone else in the state's history.

executive branch, including: lieutenant governor, attorney general and commissioner of agriculture.

A 31-member Senate and a 150-member House of Representatives comprise the state legislature that writes and passes laws. Voters elect senators to four-year terms and representatives to two-year terms. The legislative branch convenes during odd numbered years and for no more than 140 days.

A chief justice and eight associate justices rule from the Texas Supreme Court, the highest state civil court.

Voters elect justices to six-year terms. The judicial branch includes a criminal court of appeals and district and county courts.

Texas has more counties than any other state, with 254. Voters elect county commissioners to serve four-year terms. A variety of government systems—city manager, commissioners, and mayor-city council—operates in more than 1,100 cities, towns, and villages in Texas.

Because of its population, Texas sends a large delegation to represent the state at the national government in Washington, D.C: two senators and 36 members of the U.S. House of Representatives.

The Economy

Texas has been the top exporting state in the nation for more than a decade. Texas exports about $265 billion in goods each year. The state's leading exports include petroleum and coal products, computer and electronic products, chemicals, and equipment. Texas plants exported about $24.5 billion in automobile parts in 2013.

Some Famous Texans

Alvin Ailey (1931–1989) was an internationally known dancer and choreographer. He founded the world-famous Alvin Ailey Dance Theater.

Starting with a $5,000 investment, Hot Wells native Mary Kay Ash (1918–2001) built a billion-dollar business, Mary Kay Cosmetics.

Respected newsman Walter Cronkite (1916–2009) was born in Missouri but grew up in Texas. From 1962 to 1981, he anchored a pioneering television program, *The CBS Evening News*. He was long considered America's most trusted journalist.

In 1925, Miriam "Ma" Ferguson (1875–1961) became the first woman elected as governor of Texas. She served until 1927, and was re-elected and served a second term from 1933 to 1935.

Miriam Ferguson

Henry B. Gonzalez (1916–2000), born in San Antonio, was the first Mexican-American to represent Texas in the U.S. House of Representatives. He served in Congress from 1961 to 1999, when his son, Charlie, was elected to the seat. Charlie Gonzalez (b. 1945) served in Congress until 2013.

Lubbock's Buddy Holly (1936–1959) became a rock-n-roll music legend in the 1950s. His music influenced the Beatles, Bob Dylan, and Bruce Springsteen, among others. He was among the first group of performers inducted into the Rock and Roll Hall of Fame in 1986.

Current-day pop singers Beyoncé Knowles-Carter (b. 1981) and Selena Gomez (b. 1992) were born and raised in Texas.

Barbara Jordan (1936–1996), born in Houston, was a Civil Rights leader who became the first African-American woman from a Southern state to serve in Congress.

Barbara Jordan

Selena Gomez

Willie Shoemaker (1931–2003) won 8,833 thoroughbred horse races during his 41-year career, including four Kentucky Derbies.

With nine interstate highways and 300,000 miles of public roads, Texas provides trucking routes to Mexican and Canadian markets. Texas has the second-largest airport system in the world with more than 380 airports.

With 400 chemical plants and refineries, Texas produces 25 percent of America's energy. Texas leads the nation in sustainable energy as the top wind-producer. In 2012, forests generated $17.8 billion in wood products, and supported more than 130,600 jobs.

Texas continues as a leading cattle and cotton state. One of every five U.S. bales of cotton comes from Texas.

The People

The Pew Research Center describes Texas as America's "stickiest" state. More than three-fourths of adults born in Texas still live there.

Caucasians comprise 44 percent of Texas's 26.4 million population. Hispanics make up about 38 percent, African Americans 12 percent, and Asians 4 percent.

Nearly 27 percent of Texas's population is under age 18. About 11 percent is over age 65. Of people over age 25, more than 26 percent have earned a college or greater degrees and 80 percent have graduated high school.

Women own about 20 percent of Texas's businesses. Hispanics own 21 percent, and African Americans own seven percent, according to the most recent data.

The state is viewed as a Republican stronghold. Texans have voted Republican in every presidential election since 1976. Texas also ranks in America's top 10 most religious states. In Texas, 74 percent of the people report they are religious, compared to the U.S. average of 65 percent.

Major Cities

Houston is Texas's largest city and the fourth-largest city in the U.S., with a population of about 2.2 million. Houston is home to NASA's Johnson Space Center, as well as America's largest medical center. The city has 18 museums within walking distance of each other. The deep water Port of Houston, among the world's busiest, celebrated its 100th anniversary in 2014. It handles more foreign tonnage than any other U.S. port.

San Antonio, where the Alamo is located, is Texas's second-largest city with a population of 1.4 million. Five Catholic missions established by the Spanish along the San Antonio River were nominated for World Heritage Status. Military installations have contributed to San Antonio's growth. The U.S. Fifth Army headquarters is at Fort Sam Houston. Brooks, Lackland, and Randolph air force bases are also located around San Antonio.

Dallas is Texas's third-largest city with a population of 1.3 million. It is often combined with the nearby cities of ***Fort Worth*** and ***Arlington*** to make the fourth-largest metropolitan area in the United States, with a total population of nearly 7 million. Established in 1841, Dallas grew with the 1870s railroad construction. It boomed again when oil was discovered nearby in the 1930s and again in the early 1980s. After leaving office in 2009, George W. Bush located his presidential library in Dallas.

River Walk, a public park with restaurant-and shop-lined sidewalks, is popular with visitors to San Antonio.

Austin is the state capital and southern-most capital city in the U.S. It is Texas's fourth-largest city and the eleventh largest U.S. city, with a population of more than 885,000. Technology boomed in Austin during the 1990s, giving it the nickname "Silicon Hills." It is also known as the "Live Music Capital of the World." Austin is home to the University of Texas and the Lyndon B. Johnson Presidential Library and Museum.

Further Reading

Altman, Linda Jacobs, and Tea Benduhn. *Texas.* New York: Marshall Cavendish Benchmark, 2011.

Somervill, Barbara A. *Texas.* New York: Children's Press, 2009.

Internet Resources

https://www.tshaonline.org/handbook

The Texas State Historical Association provides a "digital gateway to Texas history" at this website.

http://www.texasbeyondhistory.net/kids/research.html

This page for kids, hosted by the University of Texas at Austin, has links to information on many topics of interest to students, including Native Americans of Texas, the state's role in the Civil War, geography, and other topics.

https://www.tsl.texas.gov

Texas State Library and Archives Commission

 # Text-Dependent Questions

1. Why do Texans remember Stephen F. Austin?
2. Where was the last battle of the Civil War fought? When?
3. How did Texas change after Spindletop?

 # Research Project

Former Texas Governor Rick Perry once referred to Texans as a "different breed, set apart by their fierce individualism and unyielding desire for freedom." Research the Lone Star Flag in encyclopedias and web sites. Explain how the Lone Star Flag represents Texans past and present.

Index

Numbers in **bold italics** refer to captions.

Series Glossary of Key Terms

bicameral—having two legislative chambers (for example, a senate and a house of representatives).

cede—to yield or give up land, usually through a treaty or other formal agreement.

census—an official population count.

constitution—a written document that embodies the rules of a government.

delegation—a group of persons chosen to represent others.

elevation—height above sea level.

legislature—a lawmaking body.

precipitation—rain and snow.

term limit—a legal restriction on how many consecutive terms an office holder may serve.